D1084924

Teenage Refugees From

EASTERN EUROPE

Speak Out

North
Sea

DENMARK

Baltic
Sea

ESTONIA

LATVIA

LITHUANIA

BYELARUS

NETH.

GERMANY

Berlin •

(East Germany)

• Gdansk

• Warsaw

POLAND

UKRAINE

BELGIUM

Chemnitz •

(West Germany)

• Prague

CZECH REPUBLIC

(Czechoslovakia)

SLOVAKIA

FRANCE

AUSTRIA

• Budapest

HUNGARY

ROMANIA

SWITZERLAND

SLOVENIA

CROATIA

• Voivodina

• Novi Sad

(Yugoslavia)

Bucharest •

BOSNIA and
HERZEGONIA

SERBIA

BULGA

ITALY

MONTENEGRO

• Sofiya

MACEDONIA

Adriatic
Sea

ALBANIA

Tyrrhenian
Sea

GREECE

Aegean
Sea

Ionian
Sea

Mediterranean Sea

IN THEIR OWN VOICES

Teenage Refugees From

EASTERN EUROPE

Speak Out

CARL ROLLYSON

THE ROSEN PUBLISHING GROUP, INC.
NEW YORK

Published in 1997 by The Rosen Publishing Group, Inc.
29 East 21st Street, New York, NY 10010

First Edition
Copyright © 1997 by The Rosen Publishing Group, Inc.

Manufactured in the United States of America.

Library of Congress Cataloging-in-Publication Data

Teenage refugees from Eastern Europe speak out / [compiled by] Carl
    Rollyson. — 1st ed.
        p.   cm. — (In their own voices)
    Includes bibliographical references and index.
    Summary: Teenage refugees from several Eastern European countries tell
their stories of immigration and adjustment to the United States.
    ISBN 0-8239-2437-8
    1. East European Americans—Biography—Juvenile literature.
    2. Immigrants—United States—Biography—Juvenile literature.
    3. Europe, Eastern—Social life and customs—Juvenile literature.
    [1. East European Americans.   2. Refugees.   3. Europe, Eastern—
    Social life and customs.   4. Youths' writings.]   I. Rollyson, Carl.
    II. Series.
    E184.E17R65   1997
    973'.04918'00922—dc20   96-44218
                                                                        CIP
                                                                         AC

Contents

A hunger striker participated in a 1990 protest in Bucharest against Romanian President Ion Iliescu.

INTRODUCTION

The term "Eastern Europe" is usually used to refer to the countries that came under the domination of the Soviet Union at the end of World War II. At that time, Poland, Czechoslovakia, Hungary, Yugoslavia, Romania, Albania, and Bulgaria became "Soviet satellites"—countries with Communist governments that closely followed the policies of the Soviet Union. In 1949, Germany was divided into two separate countries, with East Germany under Soviet control. British prime minister Winston Churchill described the Communist takeover of Eastern Europe as an "iron curtain" that had fallen across the middle of Europe. In every case, these Communist regimes were maintained by force rather than by free elections.

Beginning in 1989, the Communist governments of Eastern Europe began to collapse and be replaced by freely elected, non-Communist governments. In 1991, the Soviet Union itself broke up. The "iron curtain" had been lifted.

Before 1989, many Eastern Europeans fled to Western Europe, to the United States, and to other parts of the world. They fled hoping to find political asylum (protection) and freedom from harsh Soviet policies. Each new generation of young people was faced with a dilemma: Should they remain in their native land? Should they work to change it? Should they leave? Many chose to immigrate—often to the United States, where many Eastern Europeans had friends and relatives who could help them adjust to the American way of life.

A refugee is someone who flees to another country for safety. Many become refugees because of oppression or persecution. Not all Eastern Europeans felt persecuted, yet no young person growing up in an Eastern European country before the fall of communism experienced the kind of freedom enjoyed by American teenagers.

Soviet control restricted individual freedom in ways that were often brutal. In 1956 the Soviet Union invaded and occupied Hungary when its citizens attempted to form an independent government. In 1968 Soviet tanks drove into Prague, Czechoslovakia, destroying a reform-minded Communist government. Every Eastern European country has a history of uprisings against the Soviet-backed governments and a record of those liberation movements being brutally suppressed.

As the interviews in this book emphasize, children in Eastern Europe grew up learning that they had to be careful about what they said outside the home. Criticism of Communist policies, or of a Communist leader, might get a family in trouble. A parent might lose his or her job; the security police might visit one's home and question family members. Anti-Communists were followed and sometimes beaten. If you had relatives in the United States, you were especially vulnerable. It meant you might have access to information that Communist authorities wished to keep from becoming public.

Communist society was a closed society, and censorship was necessary to keep people from learning about the outside world. Yet Communist efforts to control the way people thought ultimately failed. The interviews in this book demonstrate that the peoples of Eastern Europe were eager to learn about the world beyond the "iron curtain." Young people wanted to know about their grandparents, uncles, and other family members who lived abroad. Most of all, they yearned for the opportunities that North America seemed to offer. North America was the refuge of their dreams.

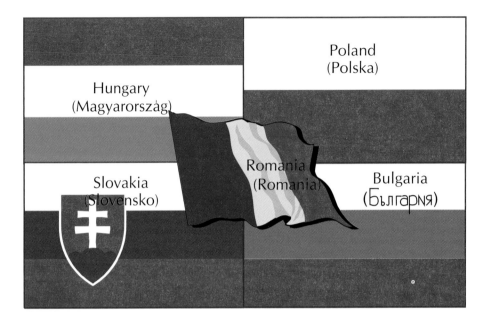

Hungary
(Magyarország)

Poland
(Polska)

Slovakia
(Slovensko)

Romania
(Romania)

Bulgaria
(България)

You will see from these interviews that much of the image that these teens had of the United States was more of a dream than reality. Once here, some refugees or immigrants may be somewhat disappointed in certain aspects of their new lives. Yet what continues to excite these young people is that the United States provides hope for a better future, because it upholds the idea of individual freedom and of achieving your own dreams.

When you talk to Eastern European refugees and immigrants, you may be surprised to find that they may have left behind fairly comfortable lives. They sometimes faced economic hardships once they reached the United States. However, the

United States offered greater opportunities to receive a higher education, to explore a variety of careers, and to express oneself more freely than in Eastern Europe.

Knowing certain political and historical facts will help you to understand all of the reasons why these young people have sought to make a future in the United States. Here, in brief, are some key events that will help you to realize why the goal of a life in America was so important for thousands of Eastern Europe's young people.

Poland

Poland is a land of nearly 40 million people, bordering Germany in the east and Russia in the north. The Czech Republic and Slovakia lie to the south of Poland. Its central position in Europe has exposed it to several invasions and partitions in its history. A German and Soviet invasion of Poland started World War II. After the war, the Soviet Union took political control of Poland, removing all non-Communist officials from the government.

After various periods of protest and unrest, a trade union known as Solidarity was established in 1980. The union posed a serious threat to the Communist government. In December 1981 the Polish government declared martial law, a policy of strict law enforcement by the military. The government wanted to stop Solidarity from strik-ing for higher wages, lower prices, and an end to censorship. Many of Solidarity's leaders were arrested and imprisoned. Although Solidarity was declared illegal in 1981, it became so powerful that the Communist government reinstated it as a legal union and political party in 1989. The rise of Solidarity has often been cited as a key factor in the loss of the Soviet Union's control over Eastern Europe. Lech Walesa, the former leader of Solidarity, was elected president of Poland in free elections in 1990. He was defeated by Aleksander Kwasniewski in 1995.

Czechoslovakia

The nation of Czechoslovakia split twice in its history. During World War II it split into the Czech Republic and Slovakia. The Soviet Union reunited the two countries again after the war. On January 1, 1993, Czechoslovakia peacefully divided itself again into two countries: the Czech Republic and the Republic of Slovakia.

Many of the industrial resources of the former Czechoslovakia are centered in the Czech Republic. One of the reasons for the split with Slovakia had to do with disagreements about how the country would develop. Some Slovaks feared that the Czechs would continue to dominate the economic and political affairs of a united country.

The Czechs outnumber the Slovaks. There are approximately 10.5 million Czechs, and 5.5 million Slovaks.

Like Poland, Czechoslovakia had a history of resistance to Soviet rule, especially in the period of the "Prague Spring" of 1968. Leader Alexander Dubçek's program of reform, called "Socialism with a human face," was crushed by a Soviet invasion.

Václav Havel, one of the outstanding writers and statesmen of Eastern Europe, led a group of dissidents (individuals who disagree with the established system) in a fight against the Communist government. He eventually became the president of Czechoslovakia in 1989 and of the Czech Republic in 1993. The Republic of Slovakia's president is Vladimir Mečiar, who was re-elected in 1994. He first took office after the fall of the Communist government in 1991.

Yugoslavia

Yugoslavia means "kingdom of the South Slavs." It was created after World War I as a nation of six republics: Bosnia-Herzegovina, Croatia, Macedonia, Montenegro, Serbia, and Slovenia. Yugoslavia, with a population of approximately 11 million people, remained intact during World War II and under the rule of the dictator Marshal Josip Broz Tito and his successors. In the early 1990s, however, the country splintered because of tensions between its three major ethnic groups: Croats, Muslims, and Serbs. The regions of the former Yugoslavia became separate countries.

In 1989, a protester in the Bulgarian capital, Sofia, held a sign with a portrait of former Bulgarian Communist Party Chief Todor Zhivkov. The bars painted over the portrait signified the protesters' demand for Zhivkov's arrest.

Why Yugoslavia broke up is the subject of fierce debate. There have long been tensions between the Eastern Orthodox Serbs, the Bosnian Muslims, and the Roman Catholic Croats, even though all are South Slavs and descendants of the same ancestors. Under Tito, these tensions were repressed. But the end of communism and the loss of a powerful central authority reopened a power struggle that resulted in civil war. The fighting included atrocities called acts of "ethnic cleansing," committed by all parties in the conflict.

In 1995, an agreement to end the fighting was reached in Dayton, Ohio. Today, Yugoslavia is made up of two republics: Serbia and Montenegro. The other four former republics of Yugoslavia are now independent nations.

Romania

Romania became an independent kingdom in 1881. The Soviets forced Romania's king to abdicate in 1947, and Communist rule was put in the monarchy's place. Romania's last Communist leader, Nicolae Ceauşescu, promoted an image of himself as a supreme, invincible leader. He instituted brutal political and economic policies. He was overthrown and he and his wife were executed in December 1989. A provisional government was then formed, and in May 1990, Ion Iliescu, a former Communist Party official, was elected. This government has been accused of persecuting anti-communists and pursuing only limited economic reforms. Romania presents an example of the difficulties that the nations of Eastern Europe have faced since the fall of communism.

Bulgaria

Bulgaria is bordered by Romania in the north and Macedonia (part of the former Yugoslavia) in the west. Greece lies to the south, and Turkey is on the southeast border. Several times in its history, Bulgaria has gone to war with its neighbors to recover lands it considered part of Bulgaria. It was ultimately unsuccessful. By the late 1940s, Bulgaria was securely under the political control of the Soviet Union.

Present-day Bulgaria has a population of about 9 million. In 1990, Communist Party leader and head of state Todor Zhivkov was imprisoned. He was convicted of corruption and abuse of power. The first non-communist leader in forty years, Zhelyu Zhelev, was elected president in August 1990. Economic reforms were introduced and the whole structure of government began to change, stimulated by a rewriting of the country's constitution. Bulgaria is considered to have one of Eastern Europe's more stable democracies.

Hungary

Hungary is near the geographic center of Europe. Its location provided an ideal meeting place for many different peoples throughout history, including Germans, Gypsies, Jews, Romanians, and Slavs. Today, Hungary has few minorities. The vast majority of Hungarians are Magyars, whose ancestors migrated from beyond the Ural Mountains in the late ninth century. The Magyars brought with them a language unlike any other Eastern European tongue. The Hungarian language is distantly related to Finnish.

In 1867, Hungary joined with Austria to form the Austro-Hungarian Empire. Until World War I, Hungary was a huge kingdom, covering parts of Austria, Czechoslovakia, Poland, Romania, and Yugoslavia. After the war, Hungary lost some of its territories. During World War II, Hungary took the side of Nazi Germany. Many of Hungary's Jews were killed.

Hungary was taken over by a Communist government in 1948. The country struggled with economic problems and resentment of Communist policies. Widespread discontent erupted with the anti-Communist revolution of 1956. Soviet forces swept into Budapest and brutally suppressed the revolution, killing 32,000 Hungarian soldiers and civilians. Almost 200,000 refugees fled Hungary during and after the revolution. Following the unsuccessful revolution, the situation in Hungary improved slightly.

During the 1980s, Hungary began to look to the West for trading partners and economic assistance. In 1989, the Communist Party voted to

When the border between East and West Germany was opened in November 1989, Germans celebrated atop the Berlin Wall.

dissolve itself. The last Soviet troops left Hungary in 1991.

East Germany

After Germany was defeated in World War II, the country was divided into four zones. The United States, Great Britain, France, and the Soviet Union each occupied their own zone. East Germany became part of the Soviet area of occupation. The Soviet zone was brought under the control of a Communist government in 1946. By 1948, the split between the Soviet-dominated eastern zone and the western zones was complete. In 1949, the Federal Republic of Germany (West Germany) and the German Democratic Republic (East Germany) were born.

The city of Berlin, located in East Germany, was also divided into east and west, with East Berlin as the capital of East Germany and West Berlin as an unofficial part of West Germany.

Because of the huge numbers of refugees pouring into West Germany from East Germany, the East Germans tightened security at the border and, in 1961, constructed a wall that divided the city of Berlin. The wall successfully reduced the number of East Germans escaping to the West, but took its toll on the spirit of a people who were separated from family members and the possibility of freedom.

By 1989, nationwide demonstrations and increasing numbers of fleeing citizens had forced the government to change its ways. President Erich Honecker and the council of ministers resigned and the government began to reorganize. As the wall began to come down, the attention of the entire world was focused on Berlin.

The two Germanies were reunified in 1991. The transition from Communism to a free market economy has created many challenges and difficulties.

The countries of Eastern Europe are undergoing many difficult changes. At the same time, Eastern European teens in the United States are experiencing their own challenging process of adjustment. The teens in this book talk about the hardships and joys of forging new lives.◆

In 1982, **Joanna** and her mother came from Poland to join her father in Massachusetts, where he was a graduate student. The family was granted political asylum. They later moved to Statesboro, Georgia. Joanna has lived in Statesboro since she was five years old. She is a senior in high school and is also taking college courses. She has visited her native land twice since coming to the United States.

JOANNA
THE NEED TO GO BACK

I went back to Poland in 1989 and stayed for the whole summer. I was twelve and in the sixth grade. I had no memories of Poland, except through photo albums. My grandfather, a sailor in Poland, was working on a cargo ship at the time. We sailed across the ocean to Poland. The trip took about two weeks, and it was amazing how much Polish I picked up. I learned Polish when I was little, but I was rusty, and during those two weeks my Polish really improved.

I lived with my mom's parents for part of my visit, and met my mom's sister. My aunt was seven when I was born, so I'm actually closer in age to my aunt than my mom is. My aunt took me everywhere that summer—to all of the castles and

Two women peek out from under a Solidarity banner at a protest outside the Supreme Court in Warsaw in 1981.

the sights. She helped me to appreciate Poland's history and culture.

I guess what surprised me the most was my family. I had been away for so long, but I still felt that I was really Polish. I didn't feel out of place there. It had a lot to do with the way my family showed me a lot of love when I was in Poland. They encouraged me to speak Polish and participate in the culture. My grandparents were very traditional. They lived simply. Everything just seemed very natural and slow-paced for them.

At that time Poland was starting to become capitalist. It was like a completely new

country. When you live in America, you take

commercialism for granted. But there was only one McDonald's in Poland. All of the businesses were really new. I think of Poland as being a really quaint country. For example, in the United States you've got supermarkets and fast food. In Poland I saw what it was like to have a town bakery and a town butcher shop, even though they were run by the government. Businesses were starting to become privately owned. Poland was in a period of transition. The shops did not yet have an individual look to them. Everything was extremely cheap. The second time I went back, prices were higher.

My aunt was nineteen or twenty when I first visited Poland. She had a lot of dreams for her future. She was more cultured than Americans would think. Many Americans have a very limited view of other cultures and nationalities. She had been to Germany and all over Europe. Yet she didn't understand the capitalist system. In America, you see how much work people put into their businesses. There, people were used to getting things from the government and not working to develop their own businesses. It was interesting to see the transformation from communism to a free market. Poles had to face the fact that things would be more expensive when businesses were privatized.

On my first trip I also went to Germany and saw the difference between Germany and Poland. In Hamburg everything was so modern. There were

The charismatic Lech Walesa led the Polish trade union Solidarity and was elected president of Poland in 1990.

many expensive shops. Change was just starting to happen in Poland. For example, my grandfather was really into fishing, and across the street there was this wonderful bait and tackle shop. You didn't see that kind of thing before in Poland. From what my grandparents told me, the streets weren't as safe as they used to be. So that had also changed. But it was still safer than any American city of that size.

I was in the eighth grade when I took my second trip to Poland. I was fourteen. The country had really changed. I know that it has changed even more in the few years since I've been there. The first time I went to Poland I noticed that my grandfather had a very strong tie to the Catholic Church. The second time I visited, he had changed his views. The Catholic Church had tried to increase its influence on the government. I think my grandparents resented that. There had also been a real power struggle with the government. Prices had gone up. Everything still seemed cheap compared to American prices, but not as cheap as before.

My aunt said, "I hope you feel a sense of attachment to Poland, and that you'll come back." Every time I return to the United States after visiting Poland, I always feel this need to go back again. That's the change that occurred in me. I would like to go back to Poland again, maybe during college or even this summer.◆

Luboš came to the United States from Slovakia two and a half years ago, accompanied by his mother, father, older brother, and younger sister. He spoke no English. Since then, he has graduated from an American high school and is attending his first semester of college in New York. He is nineteen years old.

LUBOŠ
LEAVING FOR A BETTER LIFE

I lived in Kaminka, a small town of less than 1,000 people. For high school I went to a bigger city, Prešov.

We lived in a house. My parents built it themselves. People living in villages owned houses, while people who lived in cities lived in apartments and paid rent to the government. We also had a Russian car called a Lada. It was very expensive for us to buy. Most Slovaks could afford to buy only one in a lifetime. We had a telephone, and a television with only two channels. If you owned a satellite dish, you could get about thirty channels. We got one after Czechoslovakia split into two independent countries. American programs only appeared on the satellite channels.

My father worked for a factory making fitness machines and exercise equipment. My mother worked in a clothing factory, making uniforms for the army and sports clothes.

I was in Czechoslovakia when the country split on January 1, 1993. At first everyone celebrated. People said, "Finally, we're going to separate from the Czech Republic." The Czechs always controlled industrial development. After a year or two, though, politicians were more in favor of separation than the people were.

It was easier to get to America after the split because there was more freedom to leave, especially with an entire family. Before, you could only go alone.

Before the split all young men had to go into the army for two years. When my father was in the army he couldn't get any letters from his parents who lived in the United States. He couldn't mail any letters, either, because it was thought he might give information to the U.S. government.

My father joined the Communist Party because he had to for work. You had to get a party ID and pay a certain amount each year. Belonging to the party did not help him. It only helped the Communist Party's high-ranking officials, who had many privileges. These officials received much nicer apartments and higher salaries. They had extravagant parties, ate at expensive restaurants, and could also go on vacation in other countries. It was much easier for Communist officials to travel. Other people resented the privileges enjoyed by Communist officials, but they couldn't do anything about it. If you said something against the Russians and somebody told the police, they could arrest you. You could lose your job. Many authors had to be careful about what they wrote.

I was here in New York for a summer vacation when I was twelve. They told us in school about the United States. They said it was a successful and free country. They didn't say bad things about it.

I was happy in Slovakia, but I think my parents wanted to see whether they could have a better life in America. Everyone was going to the United States and saying how good it was, so we wanted to try. Our family is happy that we came, especially since I got into college. It was really hard to get into college in my country. You had to know somebody who could help you get into the school, or you had to pay a bribe to the college officials. A friend of mine did really well in school. He had all A's, and he wasn't accepted at any Slovak colleges.

There is also more freedom in the United States, so I can choose any career I want. If you didn't get into college in Slovakia, you had to work. Some people tried for two or three years to get into college. I just got a letter from my friend; he got into college after two years of trying.

I know many Slovak people here. Some of them have been here for a long time but their

Soviet tanks moved into downtown Prague in 1968 in response to a movement for reform in Czechoslovakia. Workers and students rioted against the invasion but could not stop the crackdown.

parents are from my country. We have dance parties. I dance in a group that performs Slovak dances. We give performances for churches.

I'm going back to Slovakia for a vacation soon. My parents like it here. My father is a maintenance worker at a bank. My mother is working in a hotel.

When I came here, I didn't like it that much. I didn't speak any English. I didn't have any friends. I had left everything behind. But now I can communicate a little bit, and it's getting better and better.◆

Aleksandra came to Queens, New York, with her father, mother, and brother, when she was eighteen years old. In Novi Sad, a city in the former Yugoslavia, she studied at a high school for literature and language. She took English language classes for two years. She is now fluent in English and is a college student.

ALEKSANDRA
BY THE RULES OF
THE EASTER EGG GAME

I was born in Voivodina, a province in Yugoslavia. This province is known for having a wide variety of nationalities and religions. My family is an example of that variety. My father is a Serb, but unlike most Serbs, his religion is not Eastern Orthodox. His parents were members of a small sect called Nazarene. My grandfather was a Nazarene priest. My mother came from a Catholic family. Her father was a Croat and her mother was Hungarian.

Even though we lived in a Communist system and religious holidays were not publicly celebrated as they are in the United States, we still practiced our own customs and traditions. We celebrated both Catholic and Eastern

Orthodox holidays. Serbs are considered to be officially Eastern Orthodox, and even though we really did not have any Orthodox people in our family, my mother would prepare everything for Orthodox holidays.

I remember how much I looked forward to those days. I was one of the few kids in my elementary school class who celebrated two Easters and two Christmases. Two big dinners were prepared, one before New Year's Eve and one after. My brother and I would get presents only once, on Catholic Christmas, because it was sooner. We would color Easter eggs twice: Once at the beginning of April and once at the end. We also played a game of breaking eggs. The last person to have an unbroken egg was the winner. Muslim, Jewish, Gypsy, and other kids who never celebrated Easter all played that game. On Orthodox Easter, Serbian kids would bring as many eggs as possible, so that all the kids could play. On Catholic Easter, Croatian, Hungarian, and Slovenian children would bring their eggs. I would bring mine on both days.

Breaking eggs was just a game for us. None of us attended church. Most of our parents were lower-to-middle class, hardworking people, and most of them never insisted on practicing a certain religion. Maybe if we had been born in another place or in another time, we would have gotten a chance to cherish our customs. Still, I don't complain about the way I was brought up.

My parents, friends, and the people in my town taught me how to respect every religion, nation, and belief without prejudice.

We were not aware that this togetherness of different nationalities and religions was anything special. It seemed a perfectly normal way of living. But in 1991, political leaders started a civil war, which changed the life of every man and woman in the former Yugoslavia. Our town never experienced the horrors of the war, but we were all mentally scarred from the fighting in Croatia and Bosnia. Many of the men from my town were drafted into the Serbian army and returned physically or mentally wounded. Hatred was in the air.

My family never supported the war. Some of my parents' close friends were Muslims and Croatians. They came to our house with deep anxiety in their eyes. In lowered voices they discussed what was going on with our people. For two weeks we hid one of my Serbian cousins in our house, because he had received a call from the Yugoslavian army to join and fight in the war. After he fled to Portugal, we realized that there was no future for us in Yugoslavia. For the sake of my younger brother, who was months away from being drafted, we left everything we had. We sold our house and came to the United States in hopes of a brighter and more meaningful life.◆

Alexandra came to the United States in 1994 as part of a dance tour with her ballet school in Bucharest, Romania. She was sixteen. The two-week tour took her to Washington, Detroit, and New York City. She then decided to spend her summer vacation here with relatives. After two and a half months, she decided to stay. Her father recently died. Her mother, sister, and grand-mother are still in Romania.

ALEXANDRA
UP TO THE REVOLUTION AND AFTER

I go to school in Bound Brook, New Jersey. I can't study ballet because I don't have the time. But I am a cheerleader.

I lived in a house in Bucharest. It wasn't our house; the state owned it. That's how it was, up to the time of the revolution. We had to pay some rent every month, and we had to pay for the electricity. I think a couple of months ago they made a new law that you can buy your house.

My father finished high school and then he tried to be an actor. You had to pass an exam to become an actor. After the first time he took it, he got in a fight with the president of the acting company. After that they didn't accept him. He tried seven more times to pass the exam. He worked in a travel agency. He was also a math, chemistry, and physics substitute teacher, but after my relatives left Romania fourteen years ago, he was fired. Since it was a Communist country, you could not have relatives in western countries and still have a good job. My mom had a pretty good job, but she was fired when I was five. My dad still worked, but the jobs weren't very interesting.

After the revolution, my family got a boutique in Bucharest, and now we have two. One of them is rented, and my mom takes care of the other one. My dad came to the United States four times, and did some work here after the revolution. He couldn't leave before the revolution because he had to sign a paper saying something good about the president. He was very against communism and wouldn't do that. So that's why he couldn't come here. He was very involved in politics. He fought against communism, and because of this he faced a lot of problems.

I think it was the influence of movies like *Dirty Dancing* that made me want to come to the United States. I'm a movie nut. I also really hated the way my parents were treated. I always dreamed of having a different life. So that's why I dreamed of coming here and having a better life and education. People here can respect me for what I am. In Romania people who were not that good in ballet would get into ballet school because their parents would bribe the teachers. I really hated it. I didn't think it was fair.

A woman mourns a victim of the December 1989 uprising in Bucharest. Government security forces fired on anti-government protesters, killing hundreds.

Romanian soldiers celebrate the overthrow of President Nicolae Ceauşescu in early 1990. The Romanian army joined the uprising against Ceauşescu's oppressive dictatorship.

Until the revolution in Romania, you never heard about crime because everything was kept secret. You know the book *1984* by George Orwell? The oppressive society that it portrays is similar to what it was like in Romania. You would see President Ceauşescu almost every minute on television. Historical institutions were destroyed in order to kill the Romanian heritage. People who had the courage to speak up against the Romanian government were persecuted and beaten.

My parents tried to keep me away from the harsh realities of life in Romania before the Communist government was overthrown in 1989. I spent a lot of time with my grandparents. To tell you the truth, I didn't realize how terrible it was until I came here. I found out that my father was actually taken to Rahova, a detention center where people were beaten and terrorized. After that, he had many health problems. People would come search our house. One day my father was stopped by the police and beaten very badly. He was thrown onto the train tracks. He had to be taken to the hospital. He was away almost all the time. He had to leave the house for two weeks once because someone called to say that he was going to get into trouble and he should leave. They said that someone might beat him or even kill him.

In the United States I study a lot and work hard, but I also receive a lot. The teachers respect me

The former royal palace in Bucharest was turned into a museum after the fall of the Romanian monarchy. Soviet troops forced King Michael to abdicate the throne.

and give me the same respect that I give them. That is very important. Unfortunately, this never happened in Romania.

In my honors history class, the teacher asked me what I like about America. I think he was trying to persuade me to say something bad about America. But I said that it has been good for me. Everything I have experienced has been perfect.

I have been in America a year and a half now. I made the honor roll after a few months. I was also asked to be in the National Honor Society. My teachers are really proud of me. Last summer I went to California. That's where I would like to go to college—at UCLA or Berkeley. Of course, it might not happen, but everyone should have a dream or goal.◆

George came to the United States from Bulgaria when he was eighteen years old. He was welcomed by his sister, who had come three years earlier. George's parents are now divorced, and he lives with his mother and sister.

GEORGE
THE TURNING POINT

Everyone has a fixed idea about America and wants to come here for a better life. I have an uncle who has lived here for about twenty-five years. I never knew anything about him because it was very dangerous in Bulgaria to have relatives or friends abroad, especially in America.

When my sister came to the United States, she had finished technical school in Bulgaria, which is the equivalent of American high school and a little bit of college. What we call high school is eighth or ninth grade, and then we go to the *technicum*.

I was training to be an operator of a terminal in an artificial flower factory. We learned to operate the newest machines.

Sometimes it was hard for me in Bulgaria, because I was a wild kid and wanted to show off and talk about my uncle in America, but I could never do that. I always used to get in trouble because my family was very anti-Communist. I was not supposed to talk about the things I heard at home.

The Bulgarian parliament building is one of the landmarks in the capital city of Sofia.

When I was little, my friends and I believed in communism strongly. That's how we were taught. I believed in the system, and I thought it guaranteed me a bright future. Then I started to grow up and make decisions on my own, and see what is right and what is wrong. I saw from the movies that people in other parts of the world lived much better than we did, so I wondered how our way could possibly be better. I really didn't have any friends who would argue that communism is better than other systems.

The important thing was to be careful in front of others. Fifty percent of the nation disagreed with the ideas and policies of communism, but you just had to be quiet. You'd say something in front of a friend, and the friend would tell the police or your boss.

My parents taught me to think for myself, and they let me draw my own conclusions. If I had wanted to believe in the system, I could have done so, but I didn't. I decided I would have more opportunity in America.

It was a miracle that I got my visa to come here. That was probably one of the happiest days of my life. It is very difficult to get a visa to come to the United States, even for business. You have to prove so many things to the U.S. embassy in Bulgaria. There is a line of people in front of the embassy who are waiting to apply for visas. There were about 2,000 people already waiting on the list when I decided to apply. Applying takes about a month. Every morning you go to the embassy and sign your name. If you're not there when they call your name, you're off the list. Since the visa process is so difficult, I found someone to help me. In front of every embassy there is a guard. The guard put my name first on the list. My sister sponsored me to come here. Someone has to say you're going to stay with them and they're going to take care of you. It was also very important to the American government that you owned something in Bulgaria—an apartment, a car—to prove that you would return.

When I got to the U.S. embassy I filled out the application. An official started asking me questions about every piece of information on the application. For example, when it asked if I owned anything, I said yes, because my name was on the ownership documents for the family car and other belongings. He started crossing everything out. He said, "So who are you going to visit?" I was so nervous. I could barely speak. He said, "Just tell your sister to call me." I ran home and called her, and she called the embassy. He told my sister that I was young, and he didn't have any guarantee that I was going to come back. She told him that she wanted to see her brother before he went into the army, and that's all that mattered. I wasn't even sure if I was going to stay in the United States or come back. He told her that he needed a few days to think about it.

He never called me. I called him. He said that he needed to speak with my sister again. She called him three or four times, and in the end she was just furious. She told him that she would take some legal action. The next day, a Thursday, I called the embassy, and the secretary said, "Oh yes, your visa is here. You can come and pick it up." I ran to the embassy, and then went straight to the airlines' offices.

On Friday morning I bought the ticket. The weekend was a nightmare for my mom. Everybody started coming to the house. I wasn't supposed to tell anybody I was going, but in the last two days I had to tell my friends. I was so happy.

My dream had come true. The airplane arrived in New York an hour early. I stayed for two hours

In 1991, Bulgarians demonstrate against the influence of former Communist members of parliament.

A Bulgarian refugee boy rests after traveling with his family to Turkey.

by myself in the airport, not speaking any English whatsoever. I got scared, but I was excited by little things—candy, all the wrappers, the cars and taxis.

As we drove around Manhattan I sat up front in the car, getting a stiff neck from looking at the buildings. Everything seemed different from the movies. The buildings did not seem that tall. The streets were so dirty; everybody looked grumpy, running around. People didn't seem friendly; everybody was rushing to get somewhere. I expected everything to be brighter, like in California. I expected houses with beautiful backyards.

My father had an apartment in Queens. Compared to his little studio apartment, we lived like kings in Bulgaria. Everything seemed old and small. I thought about my ticket home. I was so sure I was going to go back.

The reason I came here was to start school. Of course nothing worked out the way we thought it would. College is expensive, and we didn't have the money to pay for it. I had to work until I learned the language. I've been here for five years, and I'm now in my third semester of college.

I worked in a supermarket for a year and a half, stocking shelves. Then something happened that was very good for me. My cousin from Dallas called and said, "Why don't you take one of those bartending courses?" I thought my English was not good enough. I thought I could never do such a thing. But my sister said, "I'll come with you." And we took the course together for six months. Then my sister's boyfriend, who worked in a restaurant, said, "Maybe I could get you a job running the food from the kitchen to the tables." I said, "Fine, anything to start." After working there for two months, I asked one of the managers if I could try working the service bar in the kitchen. For the next two years I worked as a bartender and I had the best time of my life. People were so friendly and polite. They taught me so much. That was the turning point, when I actually started liking things.

My life is difficult. I have to work full time and go to school full time. I'm a little disappointed with my life here. But I'm going to major in mathematics. I want to have a business of my own one day.◆

Bogi came to the United States from Budapest, Hungary, with her father. He returned home, but Bogi decided to stay in the United States and continue her education. The rest of her family remains in Hungary. She now lives in Oakland, California.

BOGI
THE GREAT CHANCE

Just as I was graduating from high school in 1989, my father got a job at the University of Cincinnati as a visiting professor of chemistry. Even though I had already graduated from high school in Hungary, I went to high school in Cincinnati because I didn't know English.

I had a hazy idea of the United States before I came here. I knew some Hungarians who had visited the United States, and I had also been exposed to a wide range of American movies. By 1989, Hungary was changing. It was becoming much more westernized.

I think that when you grow up in a certain situation as a child you accept it as normal. I had no idea of what was going on anywhere else. But I wanted to leave. I really wanted to travel and discover other things. I was a very adventurous teenager. When my father announced that he was going to come here for two years, it was a great chance for me to come, too.

There was no hassle. I had a passport. All my friends told me that I would not come back. I was very defensive about it. At that time I really thought that I would want to go back.

When I got here, it was so shockingly new that I didn't even know if I liked it or not. I had lived in a very urban environment with a lot of friends and parties. Then I found myself in Forest Park, Ohio, in the middle of the midwestern suburbs, in an all-white, very conservative high school. I came from a liberal family with very liberal friends. With the way I dressed and the way I carried myself, I was an oddball overnight. I wore all black—boots, a miniskirt. I had a crew cut. The other students dressed in sweaters and blue jeans, with white sneakers. They all had blond hair. Somebody told me, "I've never seen a white girl with hair so dark."

It took me about a year to learn English. It wasn't going well in high school in the suburbs. I would go downtown with my father to window shop or I would hang around in the university library. I didn't have any friends in the beginning, but I started making some immediately. I started talking in English all day.

My father went back to Hungary, but I decided to stay and study at the university in Davis, California. That was the only legal way I could stay and support myself. I felt I was not ready to go back to Hungary yet. When I left there, I had this vague feeling that I would do something really,

Hungarian rebels wave the nation's flag while standing on a captured Soviet tank during the 1956 revolution.

really big here. I felt I had not accomplished whatever I had come here to accomplish.

I have several Hungarian friends here. But for me, it is easier to make American friends. I still speak Hungarian, and I have a lot of friends in Hungary. We write letters and e-mail. Some people call me nearly every day, and they have visited me. I left some very good friends behind. My mother really misses me.

I believe in the American dream, but just like all dreams, it is not for everybody. Certain people have it. People who really have the dream have an excellent chance here, probably better than anywhere else in the world.◆

Claudia came to the United States in 1991 from a small village in the former East Germany. She was invited by an American family to attend high school in Billings, Montana. She returned to Germany for two years of education and then decided to come back to the United States, settling in Eugene, Oregon. Her parents and two brothers still live in Germany.

CLAUDIA
WHEN THE WALL CAME DOWN

Before the fall of the Berlin Wall in 1989, I could not have come to the United States. What happened was this: My brother went to the university in Chemnitz, and he got to know a German teacher from a high school in Montana. She was taking a course in Chemnitz for German teachers from all over the world. She asked my brother if he had change so she could make a phone call. From that chance meeting a relationship began between the German teacher and my family. She wrote to me, and I wrote to her about what it was like to live in East Germany. Then all of a sudden the Berlin Wall came down, and this teacher invited me to come to Montana.

I picked up English after about a year in Montana by living with an American family and going to school. When I got to Billings, I already knew a little bit of English from listening to the radio and watching movies, but I wasn't able to have a conversation. I wasn't really satisfied because I couldn't live on my own or function by myself in this society.

Growing up in East Germany, we got information about the United States from watching West German television and American shows like *Dallas*. In my family, it was not forbidden to watch such programs. In other families you could not. It depended on whether your parents were members of the Communist Party or not. My parents were not. The impression I had of the United States came from our newspaper, where there was always an article about the homeless sleeping on cardboard. I was not sure what to think of the United States. People said, "America is the land of opportunity." So I pictured something wonderful and glorious. But after living here for three years, I have to say that life is hard.

Coming from a former Communist country, I had a different vision—I thought people would have more time and money for leisure. But for the American working class that's not the case. It surprised me that here you have to work really hard to make a comfortable living.

People still say to me, "Wow, you're from the other side." It surprises me, since the wall fell six years ago. People ask me what my life was like. People always assume it was horrible. I think that's what Americans learn from movies—that the Russians were bad. That's not how life was. We had food and shelter. Everybody had a job. In East Germany, education was free. But the system only worked by fencing people up, building a wall, and letting in only certain kinds of information. People were not free. That's why Americans are happy. Many barely make a living, but they enjoy their freedom.

I am considering the possibility of becoming an international diplomat. I've got the education, and I am fluent in two languages. One part of me says, "No, I want to go back to Germany. I just want to be a simple person. I want to have a home and kids." But then I realize, "That's a lost ideal. I've become something else." Right now I'm going through a transition, getting out of school and deciding what I want to do.◆

Glossary

atrocity Act of extreme violence and cruelty.

Communist governments Governments which practice communism, wherein the state owns economic resources and determines the goods to be consumed.

ethnic Relating to large groups of people having common racial, cultural, tribal, and linguistic traits.

ethnic cleansing Policy of ridding a region or country of members of all ethnic groups but one, usually by military force.

free market economy Economic system in which supply and demand (the market) regulate what goods are produced by individuals and companies.

liberation movements Groups which work peacefully to free their countries from Communist or other types of control.

Muslims Believers in Islam, whose God is Allah and whose holy book is the Koran.

partition The division of a country into separate sections. Each section is independent and has a separate government.

persecution Harassment of groups or individuals because of their beliefs.

political asylum A status granted to refugees who can prove that they have fled their homeland to avoid persecution because of their political beliefs.

refugee Person who flees his or her country because of war or personal danger.

regime A ruling government or administration.

Soviet satellites The countries of Eastern Europe whose Communist governments followed the economic, political, social, and cultural policies of the Soviet Union.

For Further Reading

Epler, Doris. *Berlin Wall: How It Rose and Why It Fell*. Brookfield, CT: Millbrook Press, 1992.

Greene, Carol. *Poland*, rev. ed. Chicago: Children's Press, 1994.

Hill, Raymond. *Hungary*. New York: Facts on File, 1995.

McKenna, David. *East Germany*. New York: Chelsea House, 1988.

Ricciuti, Edward R. *War in Yugoslavia: The Breakup of a Nation*. Brookfield, CT: Millbrook Press, 1993.

Sanborne, Mark. *Romania*. New York: Facts on File, 1996.

Sharman, Tim. *The Rise of Solidarity*. Vero Beach, FL: Rourke, 1987.

Slovakia in Pictures. Minneapolis: Lerner Publications, 1995.

Stavreva, Kirilka. *Bulgaria*. Tarrytown, NY: Marshall Cavendish, 1997.

Strom, Yale. *A Tree Still Stands: Jewish Youth in Eastern Europe Today*. New York: Putnam/Philomel, 1990.

Tekavec, Valerie. *In Their Own Voices: Teenage Refugees From Bosnia-Herzegovina Speak Out*, rev. ed. New York: Rosen Publishing Group, 1997.

Index

About the Author
Carl Rollyson is a professor of English at Baruch College in New York City. He taught for a year (1979–1980) as a Fulbright Fellow at the University of Gdansk, Poland. He has published several biographies and articles on Eastern Europe.

Photo Credits
Cover, Marleen Daniels/Gamma Liason; p. 6, Larry Boyd/Impact Visuals; pp. 14, 18, 20, 22, 24, 30, 42, 44, 46, 52, 55, 56, AP/Wide World Photos; p. 26, Henrik Saxgren/Impact Visuals; p. 32, Teit Hornbak/Impact Visuals; p. 36, Archive Photos/London Daily Express; p. 39, Wim van Cappellen, Impact Visuals; p. 40, Alex Webster/Impact Visuals; p. 49, Leo Erken/Impact Visuals.

Layout and Design
Kim Sonsky